WISDOM FROM

FROM THE

Sea

By Anne Morrow Lindbergh

P PETER PAUPER PRESS, INC.
WHITE PLAINS, NEW YORK

Designed by Heather Zschock
Published January, 2002, by:
Peter Pauper Press, Inc.
202 Mamaroneck Avenue
White Plains, NY 10601
All rights reserved
ISBN 0-88088-543-2
Printed in China
7 6 5 4

Visit us at www.peterpauper.com

Introduction

ANNE MORROW LINDBERGH wrote *Gift from the Sea* over forty years ago. This gem of a book speaks to men and, especially, women, of the difficulty in finding balance and harmony in our lives. Written by the shore, the book also grapples with issues of relationships, creativity, personal space, and inner peace.

Lindbergh lived much of her life by the sea. As a child, she vacationed on an island off the coast of Maine. After her marriage to Charles Lindbergh and the devastating loss of their first son, the Lindberghs eventually settled on the Connecticut shore.

Peter Pauper Press has taken words of wisdom from Lindbergh's eloquent book, providing the reader with a small treasure trove to be unlocked at any time.

One should lie empty,
open, choiceless
as a beach—
waiting for a gift
from the sea.

I want first of all . . .
to be at peace with myself.
I want a singleness of eye, a purity
of intention, a central core to my
life that will enable me to carry
out . . . obligations and activities
as well as I can. I want, in fact—
to borrow from the language of
the saints—to live "in grace" as
much of the time as possible.

By grace I mean an
inner harmony,
essentially spiritual,
which can
be translated into
outward harmony.

One learns first of all in
beach living the art of shedding;
how little one can get
along with, not how much. . . .
One finds one is shedding not
only clothes—but vanity.

*The problem is not merely one
of* Woman and Career,
Woman and the Home,
Woman and Independence.
*It is more basically:
how to remain whole in the
midst of the distractions of life;
. . . how to remain balanced,
no matter what centrifugal forces
tend to pull one off center;
how to remain strong, no matter
what shocks come in at the
periphery and tend to crack
the hub of the wheel.*

The sea does not reward
those who are too anxious,
too greedy, or too impatient.
To dig for treasures shows not
only impatience and greed,
but lack of faith.

Patience, patience,
patience, is what
the sea teaches.
Patience and faith.

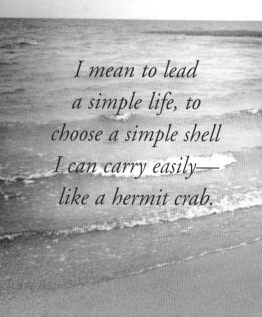

I mean to lead
a simple life, to
choose a simple shell
I can carry easily—
like a hermit crab.

*What a circus act
we women
perform every
day of our lives.*

This is not the life of
simplicity but the life
of multiplicity that the
wise men warn us of.
It leads not to unification
but to fragmentation.
It does not bring grace;
it destroys the soul.

Distraction is,
always has been,
and probably always
will be, inherent
in woman's life.

For to be a woman
is to have interests
and duties, raying out
in all directions from
the central mother-core,
like spokes from the
hub of a wheel.

*The most exhausting thing
in life, I have discovered,
is being insincere.
That is why so much
of social life is exhausting;
one is wearing a mask.
I have shed my mask.*

Existence in the present gives island living an extreme vividness and purity. One lives like a child or a saint in the immediacy of here and now.

When one is a stranger
to oneself then one is
estranged from others too.
If one is out of touch
with oneself, then one
cannot touch others.

Only when one is connected to one's own core is one connected to others, I am beginning to discover. And, for me, the core, the inner spring, can best be refound through solitude.

Eternally, woman spills
herself away in driblets
to the thirsty, seldom being
allowed the time, the quiet,
the peace, to let the
pitcher fill up to the brim.

*Solitude, says the moon
shell. Every person,
especially every woman,
should be alone
sometime during the year,
some part of each week,
and each day.*

But women need solitude in order to find again the true essence of themselves: that firm strand which will be the indispensable center of a whole web of human relationships.

This is an end toward which we could strive— to be the still axis within the revolving wheel of relationships, obligations, and activities.

*One must lose one's
life to find it.
Woman can best
refind herself by
losing herself in some
kind of creative
activity of her own.*

*Nothing feeds
the center so much
as creative work,
even humble kinds
like cooking
and sewing.*

*The pure relationship,
how beautiful it is!
How easily it is damaged,
or weighed down with
irrelevancies—not even
irrelevancies, just life itself,
the accumulations of
life and of time.*

Arranging a bowl of flowers in the morning can give a sense of quiet in a crowded day—like writing a poem, or saying a prayer. What matters is that one be for a time inwardly attentive.

A simple enough pleasure, surely, to have breakfast alone with one's husband, but how seldom married people in the midst of life achieve it.

Finding shells together,
polishing chestnuts,
sharing one's treasures:—
all these moments
of together-aloneness
are valid, but not
permanent.

The desire for continuity of being-loved-alone seems to me "the error bred in the bone" of man. For "there is no one-and-only," as a friend of mine once said in a similar discussion, "there are just one-and-only moments."

The race on the beach
[together] renews one's youth
like a dip in the sea.
But we are no longer children;
life is not a beach.
There is no pattern here
for permanent return,
only for refreshment.

All living relationships are in process of change, of expansion, and must perpetually be building themselves new forms. But there is no single fixed form to express such a changing relationship. There are perhaps different forms for each successive stage; different shells I might put in a row on my desk to suggest the different stages of marriage— or indeed of any relationship.

Yes, I believe the oyster shell
is a good one to express the
middle years of marriage. It
suggests the struggle of life itself.
The oyster has fought to have
that place on the rock to which
it has fitted itself perfectly and
to which it clings tenaciously.
So most couples in the growing
years of marriage struggle to
achieve a place in the world.

Duration is not a test of true or false. The day of the dragon-fly or the night of the Saturnid moth is not invalid simply because that phase in its life cycle is brief. Validity need have no relation to time, to duration, to continuity.

*Perhaps middle age is,
or should be, a period of
shedding shells; the shell
of ambition, the shell
of material accumulations
and possessions,
the shell of the ego.*

For marriage, which is always spoken of as a bond, becomes actually, in this stage, many bonds, many strands, of different texture and strength, making up a web that is taut and firm.

The web of marriage is made by propinquity, in the day-to-day living side by side, looking outward and working outward in the same direction. It is woven in space and in time of the substance of life itself.

Married couples are
apt to find themselves
in middle age,
high and dry in an
outmoded shell,
in a fortress which has
outlived its function.

We Americans, with our terrific emphasis on youth, action, and material success, certainly tend to belittle the afternoon of life and even to pretend it never comes.

Is the golden fleece that awaits us some kind of new freedom for growth? And in this new freedom, is there any place for a relationship? I believe there is, after the oyster bed, an opportunity for the best relationship of all . . . the meeting of two whole fully developed people as persons.

*Such a stage in life, it
would seem to me, must
come not as a gift or a
lucky accident, but as part
of an evolutionary process,
an achievement which
could only follow certain
important developments
in each partner.*

*Woman must come
of age by herself.
This is the essence of
"coming of age"—
to learn how
to stand alone.*

The two separate worlds or the two solitudes will surely have more to give each other than when each was a meager half.

*If it is woman's
function to give,
she must be
replenished too.*

[Women] must be open to all
points of the compass; husband,
children, friends, home,
community; stretched out,
exposed, sensitive like a spider's
web to each breeze that blows,
to each call that comes.

I find there is a quality
to being alone that is
incredibly precious.
Life rushes back into
the void, richer,
more vivid,
fuller than before.

[W]oman today is still searching. We are aware of our hunger and needs, but still ignorant of what will satisfy them.

. . . I must try to be alone for part of each year, even a week or a few days; and for part of each day, even for an hour or a few minutes in order to keep my core, my center, my island-quality. . . . [U]nless I keep the island-quality intact somewhere within me, I will have little to give my husband, my children, my friends or the world at large.

A good relationship has a pattern like a dance and is built on some of the same rules. The partners do not need to hold on tightly, because they move confidently in the same pattern . . .

When you love someone
you do not love them all
the time, in exactly the
same way, from moment
to moment. It is an
impossibility. It is even
a lie to pretend to.

So beautiful is the still hour of the sea's with-drawal, as beautiful as the sea's return when the encroaching waves pound up the beach, pressing to reach those dark rumpled chains of seaweed which mark the last high tide.

*Perhaps this is the most
important thing for me to
take back from beach-living:
simply the memory that
each cycle of the tide is valid;
each cycle of the wave is
valid; each cycle of a
relationship is valid.*

For it is only framed in space that beauty blooms. Only in space are events

*and objects and people
unique and significant—
and therefore beautiful.*

Island-precepts . . .
Simplicity of living . . .
Balance of physical,
intellectual, and spiritual life.
Work without pressure.
Space for significance
and beauty.
Time for solitude
and sharing.
Closeness to nature . . .

Closeness to nature to strengthen understanding and faith in the intermittency of life: life of the spirit, creative life, and the life of human relationships.

*Too many activities, and people,
and things. Too many worthy
activities, valuable things,
and interesting people.
For it is not merely the trivial
which clutters our lives but
the important as well. We
can have a surfeit of treasures—
an excess of shells, where one
or two would be significant.*

The unfinished beams
in the roof are veiled by
cobwebs. They are lovely,
I think, gazing up at them with
new eyes; they soften the hard
lines of the rafters as
grey hairs soften the lines
on a middle-aged face.

*Simplification of outward
life is not enough.
It is merely the outside. . . .
The complete answer is not
to be found on the outside,
in an outward mode of living.*

The final answer,
I know, is always inside.
But the outside can give
a clue, can help one to
find the inside answer.
One is free, like
the hermit crab,
to change one's shell.

It is true that a large part of life consists in learning a technique of tying the shoe-string, whether one is in grace or not. But there are techniques of living too; there are even techniques in the search for grace. And techniques can be cultivated.

This is what one thirsts for,
I realize, after the smallness
of the day, of work, of details,
of intimacy—even of
communication, one thirsts
for the magnitude
and universality of a night
full of stars, pouring into
one like a fresh tide.

When each partner loves so completely that he has forgotten to ask himself whether or not he is loved in return; when he only knows that he loves and is moving to its music—then, and then only, are two people able to dance perfectly in tune to the same rhythm.

Security in a relationship
lies neither in looking back
to what it was in nostalgia,
nor forward to what it
might be in dread or
anticipation, but living
in the present relationship
and accepting it as it is now.

*We tend not to choose the
unknown which might be
a shock or a disappointment
or simply a little difficult
to cope with. And yet it is
the unknown with all its
disappointments and surprises
that is the most enriching.*

*The here, the now,
and the individual,
have always been the
special concern of the
saint, the artist,
the poet, and—
from time immemorial—
the woman.*

For we are, actually,
pioneers trying to find a new
path through the maze of
tradition, convention and dogma.
Our efforts are part of the
struggle to mature the conception
of relationships between men and
women—in fact all relationships.

Who is not afraid of
pure space—that
breath-taking empty
space of an open door?
But despite fear, one
goes through to the
room beyond.

Can one solve world problems when one is unable to solve one's own?

Island living has been a
lens through which to examine
my own life in the North.
I must keep my lens when
I go back. Little by little one's
holiday vision tends to fade.
I must remember to see with
island eyes. The shells will
remind me; they must
be my island eyes.

The waves echo behind me.
Patience—Faith—Openness,
is what the sea has to teach.
Simplicity—Solitude—
Intermittency . . .
But there are other
beaches to explore.
There are more shells to find.
This is only a beginning.